The Rim Poems

THE RIM POEMS

Joseph McLeod

❦

PENUMBRA PRESS

1990

For Bryn and Elijah Harper
with thanks to Octavio Paz

Published by Penumbra Press, Waterloo, Ontario, Canada, with
funding assistance from The Canada Council and The Ontario
Arts Council.

Author photo is by Patricia Young. Cover art is by David
Maracle and was photographed for the Press by Bryan Legg.

ISBN 0 921254 22 9
Penumbra Press Poetry Series Number 24

SOME OF THESE POEMS have appeared in the following venues: Trace, Alive Press, Borealis Press, Press Porcepic, NC Press, Die Weltbüne, East Asian Review, Canadian Literature, University College of Cape Breton, Acanthus, Muse, Hartford Curant, Four Quarters, Canadian Forum, Fiddlehead, Cardinal, Quarry, Poet and Critic, Laurel, Quartet, Wormwood, Bitterroot, Edge, Proesie Vivante, North, Harrowsmith, Poetry Australia, Poetry Florida, Poetry New Zealand, Inscape, Dalhousie Review, Malahat Review, Weave, Cottonwood Review, Era, Folio, The Archer, Intrepid, Manna, Antigonish Review, Rollerskates, I Am An Indian, Other Voices, Penguin Anthology of Canadian Verse, Penumbra Press, and Northward Journal.

CONTENTS

RIM POEMS

WHEN THE MAKER OF THE WORLD completed his work, he
became aware of malevolent spirits roaming throughout his
creation. He drove them to the rim of the earth and
confronted them with their wickedness.

A battle ensued, wherein the malevolent spirits were
slammed in the face with a mountain creating the faces of the
the False Face Society. These grotesque heads—The Trickster,
Coyote—still roam the maker's world and forced by him to
work good deeds through humour and cunning and wit.

These are the Rim People and the content of these poems.

I

Moreover
I am marked by the stamp of death
great corpses
loved and dreamed on
tempters and toughs and the delicate Doorkeeper,
gestures faked and thwarted
spinning round the pieces of my furniture
filled with history's prankishness
re-immersing in dream stories
that are the flip side
of my engendering

It happens

My world banishes
brightness and darkness
It becomes heavy
with grey fog and the tops of jackpine
yet I cannot stop my thinking
and
as no one is damned alone
it goes on
and I move
between the sheets of northern stone
and become you
waiting to understand now

II

During the first round
waiting becomes the thief
and is lost in time
Next the wonder of detachment
along
with the elegance of oddness
and the strange beauty of the lie
becomes the sweet pornography
of the soul
and we say
To do a little good
we live a little evil

Poetic communication
warm and red as any flesh
becomes the witness
to a norm
seldom encountered
in any reality
and fails to explain the process
but the sun comes out

The effect of this poetry-
a day ends in the west as
a day begins in the east-
(the attention to the language
the grammar of the soul
periods and commas)
a mind suddenly gone orderly
in a natural world
sends us reeling

There are loves
that exist in a single word
These words

repeat themselves
into days weeks years
into a crystal firmness
into infinity
and deepen and become more complex
Suddenly it all
falls into visions
of sons and daughters
and the emotion is longing
for yesterday
and a simpler time that did not exist
and in retrospect
life proceeds changed
and we breath
again slowly
and determine
to work through it

III

Holding appears to become the goal
useless gold
dumb birds
plants without flowers
fields without green
never dreams
the torture of a dream
that goes beyond the second

To be drained
to will nothingness
not caring
the renunciation
of the structures of the obvious
end so that the sun may appear
the day begin

The sexual act becomes festive
a life in itself
a little living
to get a small death
Rubbing
hard and real
blind and deaf
the fun of gift and getting
at once

Now love feeds prophecy
as
truly as grazing rabbits on a hill
as marigolds in the mouths of lovers
as fingers on skin
when a little goes a long way
as sure as birdsong
as sure as winning

Learn
our bodies knew the pulse of love
before they breathed
felt need in the bone and honey-flesh
before the diamond of the eye
said
look
before the marsh of reason
found banks or rim
before our skin lifted pulse
to press and gloating soon
our bodies pulsed with love
and sang that song
in silence

IV

Fire
feel
flesh and nail
we scour the surface of our world
and find it waiting within
the naked bodies of our minds
seeking the flesh we have somehow
left behind in touching

Are we then
only to be eaten
by the wondrous complex
the sharing of
a contemptuous hardness of stone

The trees growl
as the dark curtain
of a cloud spreads
over the very sin we initially intended
(had it not been
we would have invented it
to insure our silent getting)

Metamorphoses not just change
The inner rhythm
water pebbles and sky
are equally different
and desired
love

Fire
feel
flesh and nail
we scour the surfaces
to find the joy

that existed before time
surely so now
surely so tomorrow

V

My sun turns in a yellow bed
The sun is man
Man turns in the city

Name the object by its proper
(the physical image of woman)
Establish between the union
of kiss to kiss
the bond

The sap transfused with image
as each poem becomes a recreation
a party
a ritual killing
a love-making

The words beauty and beautiful
gain power and imbued in the words
the magic mutterings of chant

(Is he aware that he is a poet?)

Dizzying words
little by little become ornaments
spin round
become the sun
my hair a halo of yellow light
lips real flower petals
soft and velvet
of a kissing god
and a loss-spitting fire
in a dark mask

These words write a gospel

Each of us eagerly desiring
this crucifixion
a forced manifest
of past
Every time we need
the spiritual lust of yesterday
in the blue waiting time
for what dream

What does one throw away
blood and birth and blind getting
What does one throw away
darkness and fear and awful getting
What does one throw away
at last the need to give

VI

Femininity was royalty
(Spouse of monarchs
consort to the magistrates of life-giving)
with a measure of phantasy
to disguise the obscene crime
concealed in the act
of perhaps
or waiting till later
or I'll do it tomorrow
as these myths
do not attach themselves cleanly
to our minds
but dream about
the periphery of our souls

The web collapsed
while I danced about the green world
The end and the beginning
revelled in by commerce and the gods
I discovered in passion
and the right surfaces to scratch

And jut as man transcends being
every other day
in blossoms and rich fish
as impossible as the magic
of human lust
as this is our state

Banality and the bourgeois burglary
of our known
became the final anachronism
as living itself
becomes meaningless
as the price of warm kisses

and life insured to the tip
in the candles to the flowers bent
urging us to talk
placing your hand just here
near my mind's core

VII

One more step and the phantoms
that hem us in
as if they were a matter
of a white shirt and a black tie
demand freedom
Shagodyweth
the Great Doctor
with a snapping-turtle shaker
explains the impossible bondage
of a true direction from government
by bankers

They say
morality is concrete
a soft mound of feathers
that flies in the breeze
like half thoughts in a storm
He says understanding begins
with the acceptance
of the failure of reason
of seeing
without eyes

It is raining
Do it
they say
We must view the negative freedom
of the tight act
Do it
they say

It is easy to cross over
Do it
says Shagodyweth
Simply to do a crude evil

you must putty a bit

They canonize their dreams of stone
while we must live out
the impossibility of living
on any green level
In the frame of history left to us
you must stiff a bit

Slightly formal in manner
always polite
sometimes playful
yet sinister in a criminal world
Elijah waits
for a melding
of solitude and peace of place
the seat of a
wonderful love

VIII

This morning is full
of mouths that lie
Each day relates
fake details
that cut ecstasy
just short of victory
not out of humility
but to establish the credence
of the mystery
of seeing a wild thing
in the woods

We were born out of women
live with women
but we die alone
heart swelling with longing
seeking
thrashing tongues
footsore

We know the mystery of day
long and disappointing
Will disturbs reason
Dreams are lost
Mystery unfolding on the obvious
and the bee
escapes from our imaginary lives
the wolf
the snake
the eagle
the deer
all realistic and impossible acts
become the obvious

It seems

we need our prisons
the maturing of harmful events
never knowing freedom

The sun will not rise
Failure is necessary
We seek it
We persist in willing it
Other men leap
into the rat-trap alone
running hard
breathing with difficulty
round and round the pressing tongue
heart swelling with longing
seeking
thrashing tongue
footsore

But what of perhaps
the victory of greening
the smiling giants
confusion
the mystery of dreaming awake
reasoning in sleep
knowing what you
finally knew always

IX

Lightness
which is precisely the effect
of the mythic body of love
Willing the sacred substance
by the power of these words
into existence
The original pariah
our existence by misfortune
found
and gloried in

In fact
it is this apparition
for an audience
the original adventure
the constellation of the debtor
the wanderer
discovering the place
where opposites agree
the order in the confusion
of this world

When we discover
that adolescence
is truly
an armed camp
the ring of the metal
the stamp of the sword
out of which comes entry
in a real world of adulthood
of fancy where we do not seem
to belong

In working from knowledge
In knowing the beginning

we construct the end
a mistaken species

If we want this love
we must scratch beneath our fingers
and let from our empty eyes
the tears of place

Each hill and each hollow
is fed
streamed beneath this body
with blood
we must present to the landscape
as offering

This body
is our body
and
this river
is our blood

X

The beauty of women-
death conquered daily
in her body-
as time out of chronological time
connects her to eternity
Asters and marigolds
crowding freely from her body
as children play forever

As soon as she fights
the sinister ravaging of her crops
as sure he must die
in each of her wars.

Her guile has given her possession
of her body
The clerks are driven wild
by her ankles
Divers seek pearls for her
at risk of like
Miners extract gold
from the heart of their world
for her adornment

The heart is elastic
The swells contract
and movement becomes life

Man is most alone
when in company
seeking completion in another
secretly coupled to himself

It follows
enough is hardly enough

and it all breaks down
this labour of the soul
the monkish cell
the memories
the dream of the past
the hope
in the beauty of women

We enter the body
seeking back
burrowing in
as a child seeking
back to know
of a paradise in darkness
a world
of knowing
the secret of the place

XI

Man spies on himself
in a desperate eagerness
to live life
as it truly is

The Beggars watch themselves
in the mirror of a lake basin
listen to themselves on the telephone
and the Thieves hear the echoing in the woods
They re-inspect the markings on their skulls

Living several lives in an invented world
of transformed theatrical props
the universe as a jail of the imagination
as
Midas turns gold into pots and pans
the sky
the grass
the children
the possibility of sustained love
into asses' ears

The function of the world is to press
between the leaves
of a forgotten book
the dry outline of a spirit
where it could have been

Perhaps we know too much
accepting and rejecting the world
save in dreams

The buzzing of a fly
against a hot windowpane
seeking out

Is it impossible to become
the thing itself
the imaginary becoming reality
pressing the hot tongue forward
to find what

No prefabricated destiny
in the same blind living and dying
allowing breath
allowing death
like a puff of air gone
the moment of the movement of an eyelash
the sudden glint of a ruby
the pressure against the mind of a thought
simple and quick and soft
as the sight of a raccoon's eyes caught
in the flash of the light

Could it be
An hour after loving
while tucking the hand of a corpse
into his coat pocket
I watch as the second hand
moves
convulsively
toward my chest

XII

The singing child in me is dead
That person I loved and adored
as a coward
turning me about like a glove
laughing at my terror
is gone

We thought so much

In the first instance
one wills disaster
to detach the soul from being

Then through the magic
we create our new world
in which we live

We slough off change
the soft moon in trees
the cool breeze
hot sun
cold water
We whistle in a green world

We love not what is
the glance
the dark eyes
the rosy legs
the mouth
but the idea
of what love
might be

Derealized
out of mind

out of being
Who would permit this love
proud soul love
tall blue foxgloves
bloodroot and all

When the moon escapes
as it prods toward
Venus in a sky block
viewed now from the sun
and we know perhaps

We cannot have the moment
and simply
it is enough

We are confronted with two images
the dream and the real

They are one
They are our lives

We live as surely in darkness
as in what light

XIII

The light faces smile
in the dark out there
The sounds of a thousand breathing
I cannot see

The knowledge that wounds
as within burned love
The questions asked quickly
Yes
and quickly answered
Yes
as I untangle the pure
and ask why the wounding
No

Once begun we soon feed on false sorrow
and consumed by desire and timidity
in a society that feeds on crime
we develop means to suffer
unknowingly pack them into
our lives like gold
and soon there is nothing left
but the sad light
feeding on itself in absence

We lose the possibility of love
of living on two levels
lost reality

Down the sharp bank to Superior
the soft movement of the sea gulls
glide invisible paths
that they know
toward an island humped with rock
and a breeze clips past my ear

whistling a song it knows
and I turn back
and find you
looking beyond me and everything I know
lost in your dreaming

There below the clouds
the dream children smile back at me
and their teeth glimmer like stars
in the soft light
There bodies as soft as clouds

They crowd into my mind
wandering down to that mounding water
and I am alone
found in dreams
more real
than your sun

XIV

Against the future freedom love
it may be objected
as Coyote loved birds
whose job it was to harm
was to allow the occasional
relieved of the functions of the child
the secret skin
wrapped tightly
round our presence in hiding

They know that we love them
but who is the real traitor
In order to be at least worthy of love
a melancholy object of passion
a dazzling light
the more violent dizziness
in the presence of unity

Loving that god
all to be for him
saintliness plans to rise
and betrays us instead
as we
wrapped tightly in our being
seek out the infinite

The comparison can enlighten
cast a spell
occupy time
betray the results
loving man more than god
loving ourselves more than man
loving the child in the child-wrap

We lock ourselves in

and busy ourselves
exact a counterpoint of place
seek out noises in answer to solitude
emerge to dream with our eyes closed
The spider on the surface of the still pond
The sudden flight of birds

We move next
toward an actual day
a real time
sweating and shouting with the dance
wild and slouching with release
we learn at last
in ecstasy
to dream with our eyes open
and use the dream

XV

Love becomes the buffer
between the imagination and the reason
a soft world membrane
a world of melt
warm secret and pulsing with love

Someone has sent her
in every object
the presence
of somebody else
something else
another place
a double image
of self

Piece by place
our life was torn away with getting
From everything we dreamed
as we floated to now
in absence
above the field of hay
the marsh
the sky

It seems the methods
apply as surely to morality
as they do to the construction
of a car

The interest suddenly becomes due
The buffer was before
the land of discovery
of the edges of fact
yet
we face

the facts
looming and obdurate
as a stone wall
with knowing

XVI

It is enough
Blood pumping
Arms aching
Coming back to look secretly
debunking my fear
going from one pimp to another
asking the questions

This day is as various
as any yesterday
as the layers of air
to the very stations of the moon

Up from the water I break surface
and crawl onto the shore
and find you there and the blue skies
and the memory of a cleft-lipped child
biting the head from a living fish
as stolid as love

Hoping again
I hold your eyes
in my cupped hands
and answer
Change

UNCOLLECTED POEMS, 1950-1960

Sweep Down Spade Deep

Sweep down spade deep
into my sweet marrow
wind
and empty out
(if you can)
the warm desire
to persist in love

Whistle down
discordant trumpet
a northern valley

Cut into the wintergreen
of time
and shatter
the leaf

Scatter the remembered
frostskate of birds
across
the horizon of white

Wind
splurge this landscape
horde-haven
waiting, wondering, wanting

Shudder down deep
as I scatter my fancies
like beached stars
exposed on sand
for any to see

Greendream

Green of time
a vine grows within my veins
and will be green of time forever
Green in the haze of poplar bend
tipped from hill to sky
Green in a pulsing earth
breathing to the same sky
within green
in and within

Without
time cracks white
out from my lips
out across the frost face fields
of winter's tight air
Out
where only promises
of summer's freedom gust
between the trees
and split like snowbirds
sparks against the snow

Out
Out
Change green and out
and in
and there my spirit sheds my body
and is green as a vine pulsing
dreams

The Earth Belongs

The earth belongs
to those who dig
who push back
their flesh
and smell the lush stink
of spring-plant buds
who see the hill tipped to the sun
who splash their eyes
with yellow light
lilac and rhubarb

The earth belongs
to those who hear
the water-runs under wind-wallows
and streaming gulls screaming
close to their world of water
Who feel the blind resistance
of the untouched jackpine
spitting back sap
to the metal bite

The earth belongs
to those who tramp
the tunnels of the town
who click the clacking mechanics
of the factory
knowing
to know the pain
and fling it up the wind
still desiring it all
as the sap runs over
and down onto the loam
that returns payment
only
in the sweet coin of life

The Truth About a Guy

You want to know
the truth about a guy
go camping,
set squares of canvas
over lichened rocks
by a wind-splashed lake
and
find out
who
cuts wood,
cleans fish,
builds fires.

Iron red water's
more a test
than blood
as paddling
you feel
the spurting bounce die
for lack of
push and punch,
and turn
back along the ribs
of a wood-flash canoe
and find a feeble paddle
in a feeble hand,

It's not what you say,
it's what you do
wet
as the tent drips night
on the third day. . .

It's what you expect
of a friend
and more;
what he expects
of you.

The Mystery of Andicove

We came by canoe to the ice green island in Superior.
The night shivered stars through the cold black sky,
sharp points of light cut to the swelling water
and scattered sparks before our path.
We came by night, having no choice, to Andicove.
The water rolled to the horizon and became sky,
and we were not sure where the Lake ended
and the sky began.

At first the dark waves did not seem dangerous
until we reached the mounding rocks of the shore.
there they silled like shifting memory, a slipping dream of danger.
Mammoth whales lying in lurk for boys in canoes
alone at night off Andicove.
The clear cold water slapped the shore and glittered,
and we were not sure where water stopped
and the shore began.

Trees, thundering spikes piercing, waiting, called us home,
marched the margins of the Island. Scattered beneath our legs
rank crawling juniper and hidden fissures caught. Out the trees
spread their scarred arms. Their skeletal white fingers
beckoning us into Andicove.
This horde dimmed and became one, closed file on hidden things
as we came, and the Island called and forbade in one motion.

Ojibway boys, feathered and marked, a hundred years ago,
in quest of manhood, beached as we beached now. . . The god,
Mishipeshoo, turned his head behind cover of spruce and cloud,
stopped his ears to terror on Andicove.

The screams mixed with wind through pines and water,
and these sounds fixed on our confusion for all time:
pine-wind, shorewater, screams of despair.

The boys were found bathed by the light of morning
tucked into trees. They died screaming but not heard.
fingers hung, hooked and beckoned to fright. As time passed,
the braves thinned to white and were lifted by the growing trees
to the scudding sky over Andicove.
It is said at night when wind-pine and wave-shore toss the sky
they become one with the braves.

We came by canoe to the ice green Island, having no choice,
but once there, determined to live bravely through the night.
We searched the trees, shore and fissures, for signs of the
dead Ojibway.
I know no more than the tale I've told.
We found no braves but the stars were cold.
The wind and waves and pines were screams
of lost boys and forgotten dreams
as real as the sound of my pounding heart.

Place

My country
is a cannibal.
It eats men.
It chews up their lives
and spits out their souls
onto the contours of its space.

My country's history
is a list of chewed men spent,
spat across the pages
of its books.

This then is that which my country
demands of its lodgers:
their precious life time,
the presentation of dreams to its maw,
the burnt offering of ethnic customs
to its national altar.

The cannibal
pays its devotees only
with the hard romance of
citizenship,
a life waltz danced
on a chill
pre-cambrian slab,
tickled by a maple,
perfumed with wintergreen,
circled by gadding flies,
but succoured sometimes,
if blessing lands can give,
with peace of place.

I Hear Canada Singing

(Sung to a hurdy-gurdy with
apologies to Walt Whitman)

I hear Canada singing
and it's a sometime swan song, sweetie
the rhythm section is Kate Reid looking back
and singing to herself in her morning mirror:

Ya! Ya! We got steam heat!

backed by Archibald Lampman rolling over
in his moldy grave:

Rattle them bones!

I hear it!
I hear it!
It's the throat rattle of
an old man I saw
washing dishes in an elegant summer lodge
and all that electric-bilge night
the old bag of bones popped
goof-balls made of kitchen yeast
into his screaming stomach:

Plop and swallow,
Gulp! Gulp! Gulp!
Plop and swallow
Gulp! Gulp! Gulp!

His worm-slug, white, bucket of a body
went out to the junkyard one sunny day.

(Throw a sheet over it, fer Gawd's sake,
somebody by the pool might see the body.)

Canada's song is
the song of the daisy-faced children,
the clicking wheels of a freight train,
the Stravinsky surprise of a screaming jet,
the steady sound of life-pumping kids,
dumping cars,
dumping plastic gobs,
dumping synthetic realities,
dumping,
dumping,
dumping;

A soundless song of the yawning of a bottomless maw,
of the sobbing, brain-splaying whimper
of a man on the sidewalk without a job,
of a sneaky door, and
a thundering, thudding, thumping galaxy of hooves
as The Indian, looking back over his left shoulder,
rattles over the sun-fought horizon.

Yip! Yip! Yip!

The song's the paradox is the soft wind
off the Pacific
blowing over Alberta
and cutting down the final mutilation
of time
as it slices across the stone of the North Shore
and smashes itself into a fury
at the Maritimes,
to slide at last
as rip-tide under the Atlantic.

The woodwinds, those high, fluting, fluttering
sounds of innocents floating over the
oompah, oompah,oompah,
of the sophisticated base, are:

the sweet hymn-voiced children
in the salty morning,
mono-motorscooter, drive-in sounds,
the clock-ticking syllables of the sporadic teletype,
the shimmer of a country morning,
the frenetic electric tickle of a city night,
the nervous giggle of a girl in line:

Silence class!
Silence!
Silence!

and the porcupines, woodchucks, snakes and squirrels
half-crushed and eye screaming in the senseless silence
of the surfaces of our
streaming roads.

The violins of this continental song
belong to the exuberant Italians:
the laugh and moan
of the rubber wheels on the glut-carts
in the supermarkets
the screech of tossed beer cans
in our fooling parks,
the mad sliding trombone sounds of breaking cars,
cars! cars! cars!
the once drone of a forgotten beetle in a tree,
the again chug and beep of the lost frogs,
the junebug sawing at the leaf of a dead elm.

The pauses in the song, the stasis,
belong to Earle Birney,
waiting for David to drop.
They're
the waiting for the bird to trill again,
the waiting for the reply at the dance
when all the girls are on that side

and all the boys on this side
and you have just walked across that gym abyss,
the waiting for the answer from he banker
when
you've just asked for an extension
of the loan you can't afford,
the waiting in the strange awake of night
when your secret fears
peek from your rolled-up socks
at the bottom of your bed
and cut into your mind
with incision sharpness and ask questions.

The song's theme?
A lilt you can take home with you?
Maybe, a million kids singing, GIMME' !
Maybe, a Diefenbaker waltz. . .
Perhaps, a Douglas fandango. . .
Or, a Trudeau stomp with a French fiddle. . .
But surely the theme must be
a continental chorus of Canadians singing,
PERHAPS!
Put it all together,
you've got
Canada,
a word that means a world to me.

Bum da day, bum, bum,
BUM, BUM!

The Work of Boys

I saw two boys
in the polliwog summer,
hand in hand,
jars in the other hands,
marching side by side
to the algae green pool.

Boot slip,
mud spatter,
laughing down the sun,
collecting frogs
before they were frogs,
searching the secret of below,
the meaning of hill,
the secret of grass,
the future of rock.
The work of boys.

UNCOLLECTED POEMS, 1960-1970

Mutual Lies

Say the days
are shorter
Wine is not as sweet
The sky lacks the blue
it once had

Say bread
is like cotton
Days whip by
(I recall a day
when I was seven
that was a full
summer long)

Say girls
are not as pretty
The country is failing

Say the air is not as sweet
Say water is not quite as wet

and
I will
lie with you
as we both
grow older

Whose Woods These Are

Over the last hill below the white village
the lights and the basin of white fog
and in the car's lights
suddenly
a cat curled unnaturally
on the ditch bank
curled smoothly in death on the soft wet snow

Down the last hill to the village
and a second cat
this time grotesquely flipping
on the snow
with a broken back

They must have been thrown from a car
she said

I'm tired, I tell her
I want to get home
It's late

I slowed and stopped at the bottom of the hill
It was sloppy ice
End up in the ditch, I tell her

I lined the car aimed like a bullet
and back noisily up the hill
to hit the ditch
Stupid, I tell her

There was no sensation no bump no sound
only the empty flakes of white snow

falling on the body of the cat
as I geared again and again to regain the road
and flipped back my eyes
to the red quiet on the snow
Don't look, I tell her

Cinderella

Alone before the fire
washed in fine ash,
eyes swimming with desire,
Cinderella adorned her hair
with a net of cobwebs
and cursed Anastasia.

She sat untangling her hair
with a broom end
and wished and wished
wished to God for change
that would make her prince bait
and
inbetween she damned Drusila.

Desire was so strong in her
she felt it pressing
against her pallet
like a succulent oyster.

At last
with a sudden fire spurt of light
she spat out a desire so strong
it wished them all,
Stepmother,
Sisters,
King,
Prince and balls,
to the bottom of the well.

She pushed aside the old woman
with her pumpkin
and marched in rags to the palace.
She wished them all back and lined them up
her eyes scattering scorn

on the effete velvets
waiting with their desires knocking;

And somehow
that night cursing became fashion,
cobwebs sought for,
fine ashes fifty dollars an ounce,
and the prince turned up her heels
and made her Queen of Bitterroot,
forevermore.

Another Borneo

On emerald close hills
that only play at being
mountains
the spread clouds seep
down to the fine bodied
Iban youth
at the river's edge

the youth bends over
the brown water of
Sungai Binatang
The water bulbs over
the shallow-crop mud
and pushes down
to the China Seas

The Seas
mother forth
the hill
the clouds
the youth
the river
and build another Borneo
below its rolling surface
beyond my view
but real and present

Civilization

Heat like a fat banana
rolls candored with sweet
white clouds
over the green desert of Borneo,

Heat, salt mother,
steamrolls over the hills,
river padi, me.
Heat, insidious fiber shatterer,
rolls over my desires,
rolls over my persistence,
permeates,
injects itself into my blood,
fills every cranny,
between the crack of my toes,
between the hairs of my head,
between memory and forgetfulness
of chill and oblivion.

At my side an Iban youth
tells me of, Ohsweetjesus!
and asks
How icecubes are made
by Mister Westinghouse.

How Will it Be

How will it be
Mother
when we meet
in white sheets
with a bit of gold
here and here

We'll play cards
and laugh at old times
and smell the Christmas meal
and bank the fire with black coal
and laugh
and laugh
before we sleep
dreaming of a heaven
trapped
only by the limits
of our dreams

Bees

Bees
do the work
of love
as yellow day
slides up
and sends them warm
about the flowers
to trip the latches
with keys
as red as tongues

Fat striped monsters
whose bodies
hold
the warm day ransom
for their love
held
in the dark cells
of their moon

UNCOLLECTED POEMS, 1970-1980

Bloodroot: II

Above the purple shore iris,
and the forbidding marsh marigold
gleaming yellow in the black swamp water,
mixed with trillium-three, tiny violets
and fiddle ferns,
the bloodroot
stands small sentry
protected white bloom within the fist
of the mit leaf,
replying with simple strength
to the death of winter.

Shaded by chokecherry trees,
mixed with tossed metal-bits
and old sky-coloured bottles
along the rock fences,
and in benediction in the hot haze
to the high Queen Anne's lace,
wild purple chicory,
black daisy eyes
and heavy milkweed clumps,
the bloodroot makes haven
in the riot of the farm's
tossed history
along the fence line dump.

If broken it bleeds.
You may finger the black mossrot
to find its bulging root
but it does not
transplant with ease,
lush with stiff morning wet

the gleaming sun
makes lace of light,
runs patterns
over the grass hillocks
to the rim
of watching bloodroots praying.

Cool Love

In the darkness I hear the moth
in the branches above the shed
moving through this night
without moon or wind

I hear the moth sing
among the dying flowers
in the vegetable garden
below this strange window

The moth sings so low
the vibration move at the speed of day
slowly across the countryside
booming
slow and low
to kindred spirits waiting

In the woods across my world
a moth sings in my silence
and thunders below the towers
that mark my tree-way

I hear the moth singing
and the dog whines
as the sounds
melt his small house

Below this farm
is a river
that pulses with the song of the moth
and it carries me to this love
cool as sliced cucumber

The Order of End

Suddenly the time was wrong
Now it became a rage of timing
of the inability to move
of the inability to recall
not enduring
not wearing slowly out
as the ice covered trees
slide slowly down
to the winter's burned grass
not as a signal for waiting green
no

Yes
suddenly the timing was all wrong
and before we could learn the rhythm
the beat changed again
and the body moved off
calling
no

then we recalled we never moved
we never really moved
we did not move as we had expected
as they led us to believe
but swarmed like clouds in a basin
yes

the remaining questions
will the trees free themselves
from the ice
will blood transfused free the body
from the scattered change

The word and body
breaks into parts

hands and feet
eyes and ears
members float off
out of time into digression
and quickly control is gone
and life ends all in a heap
yes

Under the twist
of brown branches
the birds drop their shadows
and sing to them

Die Heilige Schrift

Close the black book
Turn off the lights

The bars on the church windows
are not to keep the devils out
but the angels in

We nail people
to things
every day

Christ
in the streets
would bring it
all down on us

Don't worry
He knows his place
He needs us

Who can discern
white on white

It is the blood smear
on the snow
that really counts

How Does it Feel

They murdered Schleyer
He was a slightly fat man from Cologne
puffed a bit with good living
staring out from a photo
with the number: 13:10:77
below his chins
Behind him
a star and circle
and the letters RAF

Not much for fifty-five years
of demanding
yes

They car-snatch you
at any moment
i.e. walking from your patio
in Erfstad-Liblar
to the black Mercedes
and
What the hell do they want

Who the devil is
Annerose Lotman-Buckler

Are they paying us back
Are they killing us
for the life and the red roses
What do they want

Is it the bonfires
and the burning books
the neat rapier scars
and the soft-crooked smiles
What the hell is Consumerterror

Sorry children
We cannot give you that
even with a bullet

That you must purchase

In our world of history lessons
where bodies are cheap
and found casually in car trunks
and minds are cheaper
bought and sold

How does it feel

The Simple Dead

Hiking near Pfaffenberg
with my new boots
and pants from Loden-Frey
we came upon a triangle of land
about as big as a houselot

It was pocked with six-pointed stars
all askew but packed tightly
in lines
that disguised their crooked hundreds
(Not like the usual German graveyard
which is always a model of neat care
with stone walküren
and neat blankets of evergreen
and one small yellow mum
placed exactly there.)

It seems that when the Allied troops
came dangerously close to the camps
the sick and dying
were herded out into the roads
toward the Bayriche Wald
in hopes they would die spaced
under the trees
and
in the gullies
and be confused
for the simple dead

But when the smoke
blew over the fields
and skimmed away
the Jews dead
looked just like the Jews alive
and so were sorted out

and brought back to Pfaffenberg
not as a reminder
not as some weird pointer
but
just so
as it did not work

Wild in my Mind

Your sun
crazy with power
crazy in my mind
and my clouds
that curl likes toes
in disbelief
when you say such
and I say when
You say if
and I repeat nonsense
and we are totally
at difference
and the sun comes back
and I begin again
and say how
and you reply stop shouting
and I realize
we are again at the end
and
you say silence
and I say speak then
and you scream silence silence
and your sun comes back and clouds roll in
and I am wild in my mind

Ezra Pound at Colonos

Eye sockets bloody
full of flies
Twitching hands out seeking
(roadsigns are seldom in braille)
I waited for his arrival
on the highway

But when he arrived
Mussolini was on his back
and they had
smashed out his brains
and
silence filled the cavity
of his mouth
like a dusty bat
I knew he'd be no help
so I went on alone
and he to Venice
and he never even tried
to remind me
that we both
had daughters

Emily Dickinson: a Serious Syntactician

The daisy
enters
eye of feeding cow

The cow
enters my eye
and dwells a time

The unity
of daisy, cow and I
is all I know
of divinity
but
if I close my discarding eye
and banish
all the three
at once
the total
sense revolves
capricious deviltry

Milton Acorn

Milton Acorn
thanked me
for being myself
and let his eyes
spill across the floor
of the small theatre
just before
he did his rooster dance

He had tasted his blood
and the crazy posturing
and the wild condemnation
of the bum-fuckers
of this world
filled the students
in the audience
with befuddled joy

Milton was unable
to complete a single poem
Not one

Everything had become
a wondrous jumble
Shards like Ming dreams
came screaming
out of his crooked mouth

What else could we do
We smiled
and wished he would act
like a normal poet

To his credit
filled with the ecstasy

of his dreams
Milton Acorn
became his poem
and screamed us all down

Pat Lowther

We have built this
glass cage
and we have placed
ourselves
in it
to gaze out at the world

We sit in the glass cage
and wonder
why
we do not revel
in that pleasure

There is no answer
but in ourselves
In ourselves
is the shock of discontent
and more
the need
not to love
not to clutch to us
with talons
the small mice
offered in way of solace

Outside the cage
is only mystery
the story
the book
the meeting

It was at this point
Pat Lowther
went down to the heavy blows
and found her fingers

clutching mud along the creek bed
and found her mind soaring free

UNCOLLECTED POEMS, 1980-1990

The Chinese Circus

A ramp snapped up
flooding us with light
smothering us with smoke
and the danger of a mob out there
We cheered

Lumpen scrambled up
browns and greys
with masks like human faces

Their eyes could move
pressing against me

Lights cut the smoke
seared to my eyes
circles in circles
and I lift my head
and find
I am a flame
in shoes that finger a wire
I have an umbrella
quivering in my hand
like a rainbow

Their minds press forward
Nibbling at my costume
What is this?

Music fills my head
 and there is a slight nudge
Move, somebody hisses

I am on the wire
pressing against their eyes

The same voice hisses,
Move, you are the Chinese Circus!

The Salesclerk

Responsibility
like a worm in the eye
is to smile
because we do what
we said we would: pimp
The responsibility
is to smile until five
even if
we cannot keep the lids: suck
a ton of flesh
from sliding shut
Nylon, not teflon, I said!

We stretch up and shake
Cream caramel!
and think of hot coffee
and another customer slides by
like a demented eel.

Our foot's asleep.

Our arms are cramped!
Our lids
squeeze worms on paper
and we know
our day is nothing more
or less
than this body
this time

Our stomach cramps
20% off everything!
Where's the pencil?
The eels slither by
Cash credit or cheque?

We untangle our lines
and toss out a smile
and reel you in
giddy with the happiness
of purchase

The Little Girl and the Bear

Laughter bubbles from your throat
as the sun goes behind
the black bear

The clouds obscure what once
appeared to be a path
almost as straight as the heart's memory

Why is it when you see them coming
they are always almost gone

Shuffle a toe and bow to the bear
He sees us

Little girls with soft brown hair
there will be a time
carrot's magic spark
At that time
the boy who would not feel fear
will come to become the old man in the moon
smiling behind the branches
into your heart that is a mirror
of just you
now very old

Do not say then there was no joy
We should have been born warm dogs

Little girl perhaps just two lives
are enough to know
and sing of love
in the sunlit grasses of a world
Where
little girls dance and sing the endless days
while watching

the black bear's
magic

For My Son

An Inuit incubator
for a premature baby
consists of the skin
of a sea bird
stripped whole
pulled inside out
feathers within
tightly sewn

The tiny newborn
is carefully placed inside
and hung high over an oil lamp
with a tiny flame

For days
the warm child
amazed by brilliant feathers
tickled by down
in his infinitely soft cradle
is fed with milk drawn
from its mother's breast
through the inverted head of the bird

In this way
some children are born twice
suckled and survived
into an antic world
part man/part bird
special and apart

This child dreams and walks
his feet just slightly lifted
above the pavement
His eyes see the world
from heights undreamed,

all things sparse and small
aspects of our world so large
we cannot imagine their edges

In this way the child is prepared
to go into spaces and times
I fear and will not know

Change

My life is filled with sudden change
and alarms of total ruin

The bank phoned

Your brother phoned

Your dead mother phoned

What do I have to do
with Bell Telephone

The college phoned

Mastercharge phoned

God phoned yesterday
and reminded me of a promise
I made when I was fourteen

There are kinds of loving
He reminded me
that are spiritual
and transcendental
but yours
he said
reminded Him of his Father's

Can you imagine
he screamed
How the trees would appear
if suddenly
you were no longer blind

Find Me Praying

On God
I would touch you once
Slip my finger
into your eternity
and love
and love
myself
into your presence

I would forget
I lived and hated

Find me
lost among the living
and wring surprises
from my tongue
so that something
gives me just eternity
in your paradise
so lavish

So I will know
the last of it
of the Fatman with the Kodak

Click

Shorter Chinese Lyric
Wang Chi
Passing the Wine Seller's

When night comes
I am ever drunk
It is not
that I need oblivion

But when all men are drunk
with insensitivity
sobriety
is folly
too

Shorter Chinese Lyric
Tu Fu
Longing

This night at Fu-chou
moonlight in her chamber
she alone looks out

In the sweet mist
her cloudlike hair
is damp
her jadelike arms
are cold

When shall we two
against the curtains
next
with the moon showing
the dried tearstains
of us both

Shorter Chinese Lyric
Yuan Mei
A Chance Walk

Yesterday
I walked without
direction
and found
an early violet

Who can it be
who carries the news
Already
a bee
was there

Shorter Chinese Lyric
Tao Teh Ching
The Path

Travel the path to the end
Remain silent
even though all gyrate noisily

I have been there and back
Everything returns
to you

This is called Finding Silence
The way is called Destiny

It always happens
To know Destiny
is to know Silence

Not to know this Silence
is to live in Chaos

Justice belongs to Kings
Kings belong to the Gods
The Gods are eternal

Although
the body decays
Man never dies

Waking at Night Alone

All spread across the night
I find my arms this way
my legs wrapped
crazily in white sheets

But I cannot see
I cannot hear
I listen instead
to the dream just lost in waking

Slowly my mind arrives
at a sense of fear
but my eyes are not yet ready
or
are the lights out
Where is everybody?

The plant by the window
comes into view
Some sounds of water

Who's there?

Now my leg untangles
My hand becomes a living thing
and gropes towards a reality
in this world
in which I am surely dying

I touch the luminous clock
and feel
the transfer of its pulse
to my waiting heart

Birth Again

The stuff of poetry
Back from a walk
with shapes as real
as blue sky

The music has gone
out through the streets
and our hearts
all filled with cars

The bearded man
who begs in rags
near the church steps
spat on my shadow

I smiled at a child
and my face
grew very long

I was suddenly
in the body of my mother
waiting birth again
and knew
even from that place
life would be a kind of murder

Stamp on the book, somebody screamed,
easy passage denied and pull

Elijah: Tuesday, June 12, 1990

Two young guys were sick

Through the smoke and dust
you could see green soldiers and black rifles

Harper stumbled out of the door
A soldier placed a pistol into Elijah's mouth
and blew the top of his head out onto the street

Harper placed a rifle against his own shoes
as a drunken soldier ran up the stairs
An explosion threw the top of Elijah's head
out over his forehead and through the shattered window

Within the crowd of fleeing politicos
Peterson, Chretien, Mulroney, Filmon, Wells, Bourassa
Harper fell down the steps into the splayed arms
of a soldier
who popped a grenade into his mouth
and spread his body all over the wall

Met with a mysterious accident at Sucker Lake
during a military coup

Died of smallpox in Moscow at age thirty-two

Drowned in a bath at age two

Accidently smothered at birth
with his umbilical wrapped
about his throat
His baby's fist holding forth his living heart

Heart of gold
Light of the people

Wings like a feather duster
Bread and salt
Blood and sand
Earth of the world
Compassionate flesh
Light of the sun
Oka

THE RIM POEMS take us into the world of the aboriginal fallen
titans, the Rim People, who bring us along through guile and
cunning to the point of choices: the world in which we live or
the world we imagine possible, the reality of imagination or
the fantasy of reason, the acceptance of mortality in nature or
death in a civilization filled with intellectual debris.

JOSEPH McLEOD
RIM POEMS

PENUMBRA PRESS POETRY SERIES NUMBER 24
ISBN 0 921254 22 9

$9.95